RAISED by Humans

poems

Deborah A. Miranda

TIA CHUCHA PRESS

ISBN: 978-1-882688-50-0

Book Design: Jane Brunette
Cover art: "The Unknown Gate" by Anita Endrezze

Published by:
Tía Chucha Press
A Project of Tía Chucha's Centro Cultural, Inc.
PO Box 328
San Fernando, CA 91341
www.tiachucha.org

Distributed by:
Northwestern University Press
Chicago Distribution Center
11030 South Langley Avenue
Chicago IL 60628

Tía Chucha's Centro Cultural & Bookstore is a 501 (c) 3 nonprofit corporation funded in part over the years by the National Endowment for the Arts, California Arts Council, Los Angeles County Arts Commission, Los Angeles Department of Cultural Affairs, The California Community Foundation, the Annenberg Foundation, the Weingart Foundation, the Lia Fund, National Association of Latino Arts and Culture, Ford Foundation, MetLife, Southwest Airlines, the Andy Warhol Foundation for the Visual Arts, the Thrill Hill Foundation, the Middleton Foundation, Center for Cultural Innovation, John Irvine Foundation, Not Just Us Foundation, the Attias Family Foundation, and the Guacamole Fund, among others. Donations have also come from Bruce Springsteen, John Densmore of The Doors, Jackson Browne, Lou Adler, Richard Foos, Gary Stewart, Charles Wright, Adrienne Rich, Tom Hayden, Dave Marsh, Jack Kornfield, Jesus Trevino, David Sandoval, Denise Chávez and John Randall of the Border Book Festival, Luis & Trini Rodríguez, and others.

MANU NISH U-KUSKITAPANASI XUNOSX'IM
MISLAYAYA KOLO

for my little Turtle Girl
I love you very much

I'APA XUNOSX'IM

CONTENTS

Alphabet of Lies / 7

HISTORY

Ancestors / 11

L.A. Beatitudes / 12

Directions / 13

Whose Good Night? / 15

Petrology of Fear / 16

Oral History / 18

Raised by Humans / 20

My Mother Plays Solitaire While I Lay Awake
in the Next Room Waiting for the World to End / 22

Mnemonic / 25

Indian Country / 27

EDUCATION

Poverty 101 / 33

$10/hr / 35

Swimming Lessons / 36

The Aubade's Apprentice / 37

Clementines for Beginners / 38

10 Things I Know About Betrayal / 39

Quickening: A Catalog of Desire / 41

Primitive Uses for Poetic Forms / 43

Eating a Mountain / 45

Marriage Proposal / 47

Wolf Lullaby / 49

FAITH

My Father Talks to God / 53

Java Woman / 56

What We Save / 57

Elegy For My Grief / 58

Blessing the Doubts / 59

Dulles Airport, Sunday Night / 60

Rosary / 61

Stones / 62

Some Years / 64

Why God Made So Many Crows / 66

Faith / 67

Decolonizing the Alphabet / 69

Acknowledgments / 73

About the Author /

The Great Lie is that this is civilization. It's not civilized . . .
Or if it does represent civilization, and that is truly what civilization is,
then the Great Lie is that civilization is good for us.

– JOHN TRUDELL

Alphabet of Lies

Covetousness is both the beginning
and the end of the devil's alphabet...
                    - MICHEL DE MONTAIGNE

Anthropologist lies advertising certificates of authenticity.
BIA lies breeding bastards nobody wants to claim.

Casino lies cozy as road-kill in the beak of a crow.
Drunken lies dying in ditches.

Easy lies eloping with your everything.
Flashy mother-fracking lies breaking your heart.

Guilty lies grinning like guns.
Hungry lies swallowing houses like sink-holes.

Imaginary lies insisting the invasion was just bad press.
Jaunty lies lighting up a joint at desecrated graves.

Kinky lies strutting black Kevlar boots all over your water rights.
Lame lesser-of-two-evils lies - just following orders.

Monstrous lies getting off on a good mind-fuck.
Nasty lies tattooing your CIB number with dirty needles.

Official lies obliterating history like a chainsaw through ancient oaks.
Pretty post-colonial lies puckering their way out of prosecution.

Quiet lies quelling questions: quit while you're ahead.
Raw lies reaping parasites, and reason.

Sorry-ass lies claiming sobriety, singing like a DUI.
Toxic lies mutating promises – think treaties.

Ugly lies faking ululation under unnatural feathers dyed in China.
Viral lies ventriloquizing the voices of Vatican victims.

What-you-don't-know-can't-hurt-you lies playing war with trust-us-just-sign-with-an-
X lies.

Yawning lies stretch out, yyyyyyes, they voted for your federal
    recognition.
Zombie lies zig-zagging through generations like contagious zygotes.

Learn the drill. Teach your children:
Alphabetize. Civilize.
Reservation. Termination.
Savage. Savage. Savage.

one

History

Ancestors

We belong to the sea. We are salt water walking on the land in soft containers called flesh. Chloride, sodium, sulfate swim in our veins, warm and elemental. Our bodies sway and swell in response to the tides of our oldest memory. The moon pulls the sea, the sea pulls us. Walking on two legs far away from the birthing waters, we travel wide plains, rest awhile beside icy streams, make shelters out of snow. Always, we seek water, wherever we go, look for lost relatives, pieces of our selves. We smell wetness beneath rock; we raise our faces to gray skies, mouths open; we welcome the fat drops with our thirst. We belong to the sea, we bear her dark green wishes and slippery strands of thought. Magnesium, calcium, potassium slide through our veins. We make love to each other, oceans aching to reunite; homesick, we ease our isolation with each other's moist mouths, secret seeps, lonely seas meeting on our slick skins. We belong to the sea: she makes her claim on us in the end, demands our return, asks us for her copper, her cobalt, her molecules of hydrogen, oxygen, iron, bicarbonate, bromide, strontium. We leave flesh behind us on the shore, husks that dry and turn to dust. We slip into the sea like a child to an embrace, like blood to blood. We give it all back. We go home.

L.A. Beatitudes

Blessed is the cereal bowl with a crack down one side,
for it is a hollow center, filled. Blessed is your favorite spoon,
tiny forget-me-nots scrolled on the handle. Grandmother's
old plate with a fluted rim holds this story together.
The winged creature in the corner trying to hatch out

of a small box is your older sister, trapped in a fairytale
gone dark. The little boy in a Superman cape refusing
to eat his peas is your brother; someday, he'll save
himself. This is the blessed varrio, dressed up
by black mascara on La Virgen's elegant lashes;

she hangs crooked, guarding bruised spots on the rug,
pale raised rings on the coffee table. Your daddy's
Tres Flores anoints you long after he is taken away in handcuffs,
and TV shows- Howdy-Doody -- American Bandstand --
Star Trek – become your first religion.

Tonight your mother wanders between
shadows after midnight, smudges your siblings
with ash and smoke, touches your cheek
once. She seeks the crooked maps of dreams.
Her heels click out the front door, down the hallway,

out into the street. The refrigerator motor switches on
like a lullaby you won't remember. In the morning
the new world will begin. In the morning you'll learn
a new song: the stranger's blessing for orphans.

Directions

Our DNA is a map
made of stories.
A genealogy
of storytelling
festivals, featuring
the belly laughs
of ancestors,
babes yet in the womb,
and those looking
at us through eyes
not yet made
of stardust.

When we tell stories
we tap an ancestor
on the arm, ask
her to speak. We
take the hand
of a child, let
our fingers intertwine.
We time travel
in a curling wave
that crashes
and crashes
on the shores
of our flesh.
Damn, we are fine
grains of sand,
swirling kelp,
all the luminescent
plankton that ever swam!

When we tell stories,
skeletons dance
in dark museums,
clappersticks crack
like lightning deep
in unmarked graves.
Abalone beads shine
like oceans. And I am
an abalone bead,
drilled true, strung
on twisted fibers,
one of many
glowing jewels
on a strand that spirals
round and round
like the Milky Way.

Tell me a story.
Tell me how it happens.
Tell me a tale
my bones
can't forget.

We are beloved
bodies of work
dancing a spiraled
flight path made of words,
ink, tongues. We speak
a bright language
with no word
for dead, or end,
or lost. Following
these constellations,
we will always
find our way.

Whose Good Night?

AFTER VIEWING THE PAINTING,
"JESUIT MARTYR-SAINTS OF NORTH AMERICA"

The Jesuits do not want to go gentle into their good night
even though it's the fastest way to martyrdom and halos;
they hold up crucifixes to show they're in the right.

Those wise men stand firm, let the tomahawk take a bite,
say their prayers at the stake as flames nibble their toes
but they'd rather not go gentle into God's goodnight.

Pierced with Indian arrows still full feathered in flight,
struck dumb by wooden warclub's brutish blows
they hold up crucifixes to show they're still in the right

See, already they ascend into heaven, a glorious sight
treading soft fluffy clouds with their heads all aglow;
already it's worth it, going so gently into good night.

Brave men far from home, faith your only might
Let go, let God, above all let baptismal waters flow!
Hold up your crucifixes of gold to show you're in the right

Attend your Father, your angels, look down from new height
Forgive us, we're savages made simply, from clay.
We refused to go into colonization's good night.
We gave up our bodies, we're martyrs too, right?

Petrology of Fear

Fear is a quarry –
granite, marble, quartz –

speckled with fool's gold,
buried beneath an old mountain,

caressed by time's cold fingers.
Dig or blast or hammer down

to secret springs, baptize
yourself in black water.

Fear sings to us in gravelly,
crushed notes. Decorates itself

with spiked fossils of shells,
impressions of prehistoric desires

caught in epic accident. Fear hunches,
meek round stone in a garden,

one gray side overgrown with lacy
green moss, perfect missile

to shatter the clear pane of glass.
Fear breaks like chert, sprouts

a sharp spiny face -
slices your lips with a kiss.

Fear smells like wet slate,
ready to break and split,

silky bare with darkness,
eager for white chalk confessions

scraped with a wild hand
on its newborn skin.

Oral History

You missed out on Benny.
You weren't born yet.
He was one of Mom's real winners,
Mexican guy, a gang member
with tattoos and a big knife.
He used to grab Jamie
by the hair,
throw him
across the room.
My job was to catch
the poor kid
before he hit
the wall.

My sister tells me this
from her hospital bed
fifty-odd years later,
recovering from another surgery
related to her Vicodin
abuse. Our mother's ashes rest
a few miles away in a small crypt
at Inglewood, near
the tiny box
containing our other sister,
the one who didn't
make it out. Hundreds of miles
to our north, Jamie heads
downtown for his daily dose
at the Methadone clinic.

Did you know,
I ask my sister, that brain injuries –
actual holes in the brain –
can be caused purely by
emotional trauma?

Eighty-nine pounds
of survival, she looks
at me with our mother's
huge blue eyes.

No shit,
she says.

Raised by Humans

My mother abandoned me.
Left me behind, didn't look back.

She had lovers: Alcohol, Heroin, Despair –
followed them far up the coastline from our homeland

to the interior of a strange place: dark green firs
and man-made lakes full of jagged stumps

rising out of the waters that drowned them.
My mother abandoned me, but my aunt and uncle took me in.

They bought me clothes, bathed me, fed me every night.
I waited for my mother to come back.

It wasn't the first time. But it was the hardest.
She finally showed up with Trickster/ Con Artist/ Coyote.

Together we rode off in his white pick-up truck
north to the rain. They locked me in a tin house,

went carousing while I huddled each night alone.
Sometimes I escaped to surrounding woods,

ate huckleberries and drank from a muddy creek,
slept buried in dried pine and cedar needles. But like a tamed fox

I always went back to my captivity for dinner, begged
for a crumb of something.

Sometimes I got it. Sometimes I wolfed
a meal down greedily, not caring who saw my starvation.

Sometimes the bowl was empty – nothing, no one,
and I hung around waiting, whimpering, chained

to my cage by a metal only the human heart
knows how to forge.

My Mother Plays Solitaire While I Lay Awake in the Next Room Waiting For the World to End

She plucks out The Joker
in his floppy red and black
hat, sets him aside like a naughty child
sent to sulk in the corner.

The rest of the deck
ripples in the heart-shaped
embrace of her hands.
I love the way she shuffles,

shiny cards arcing up into
curve between thumb
and forefinger;
perfect cuts of paper

obey her like soldiers,
ruffle into a sound like satisfaction,
like control. She shuffles
random, shuffles chance,

shuffles luck.
She bangs the deck
on the table, two,
three, four times, cuts the stack

like a slab of butter, bangs again,
her gavel of judgment.
Ready.
Deals off the top,

one,
one two
one two three
one two three four

all facedown, hidden,
mirror-twin bicyclists
peddling like mad --
then the starter card, face up:

fat moment of fate hanging
between what could be, what is.
My mother's totems
are red and black,

hearts, spades, clubs,
diamonds, slick ritual
of spells against desperation.
She works with what

she's dealt: thumbs three cards,
slaps down, makes use,
makes do. Three more.
And three more. Threes

and threes like the Father
the Son the Holy Ace
as if her life and the lives
of her children and grand-

children depend on these
hands shuffling, dealing,
thumbing, slapping, banging.
As if my mother saves the world

card by card, game
by game. She knows if she
loses it only lasts until the next
shuffle. Knows if she wins,

the game's never over.
Some women knit their
sanity together every day
with yarn and the clackery

of angry needles. Some women
solve crossword puzzles.
Chain smoke Pall Malls.
Whatever witchery makes

a way to carry on: go on mothering,
grandmothering storms that
will not calm, brokenness that cannot
heal. My mother plays solitaire,

ignores The Joker she's exiled
temporarily. Soon, she knows,
she'll have to let him back
in but for now she shuffles,

shuffles, shuffles cards, a sound
like wings, like time being killed,
like the odds will be better
tomorrow and I lie in my bed,

learning the art of prayer.

Mnemonic

I was born on the San Andreas Fault. I carry
that promise of violence and destruction down
the center of my body like a zig-zag of lightning.

My father was born there, my mother too,
all my brothers and sisters. Sometimes I think
that's the only thing we still have in common:

our emergence on the edge of a rippling continent
where the sun goes down over warm waters;
born in the desert's shadow, between

mountains and sea. Some of us got into cars,
drove north on long interstate freeways.
Some of us stayed not twenty miles

from our birthplace, bound by love or hate
or fear, unable to imagine a sunrise
without palm trees – or sun. Some of us

died, turned to dust inside incinerators
built for human flesh; our ashes tucked
in a niche at Inglewood or scattered by children

on the green currents at Tuolumne. Some
of us no longer speak to one another, silent
as rusty knives; others learn old languages,

make new songs out of scraps. Some of us
journey only in motes of dust shining
above the fractured chasms of earth.

And some of us return in solitary dreams
to sacred places we could not find
in this lifetime. Today, I wind a string

of shells around my wrist four times,
a bracelet strung so I can bear
the beauty of my homeland with me

wherever I go. The sharp edges bite
my skin, rattle soft as pebbles as I write
these words. Abalone hangs from my neck:

polished shards of oceanic memory.
I was born on the San Andreas Fault.
I carry that rattlesnake in my spine, feel

the plates of a restless continent grind
and shift from tailbone to skull, a tectonic
rosary that keeps coming unstrung, keeps me

tied to the plundered bones of this place.

Indian Country

FOR JOHN T. WILLIAMS, AND ALL INDIANS LIVING ON THE STREET

1.

On Broadway or 1st Ave, on Capitol Hill
or Pioneer Square, the Indians gather
in doorways or benches or grassy bits of park.
They sleep, sell Real Change, tell stories,
carve little totem poles, share cigarettes,
wait for the bars to open –
for the shelters to open –
for the soup kitchens to open
wait for the world to open.
This is Indian Country, potholed streets
Indian trails leading up and down steep sidewalks;
Indian graffiti, scars
across the faces of men
from old families of carvers,
women from clans of basketweavers,
all falling out
of the American Dream.

They call me sister when I walk by:
sister I'm a long ways from home
sister you look like my Auntie
sister ya got a spare smoke
sister take this, just a little gift,
sister can I give you a blessing?
Their breath smells like the beer bottles
from my childhood. Beautiful hair gone
spare and silver, eyes vomiting all
the scary things about being Indian

that I ran real hard to leave behind,
tried to hide under the stink of my shame.
If I say no, they wave me on with a shrug,
if I give them money they assure me they won't
spend it on drink,
if I stop to admire
carvings or drawings or beading
they stand silent.
They never say the word 'buy,'
just, 'Whatever you think is right sister.'

I don't give as much as I might;
afraid mine could be the fatal dollar
that keeps them out of the shelter
or lands them in the morgue.
I give enough
to ease my conscience,
get them through another hour.
I know I'm feeding the meter
of Colonization,
paying the rent on a parking space we should own,
but I can't keep them safe,
I can't keep them warm or sober or clean.
I'm not a good sister.
I'm not even a good Indian
and this isn't survival.

2.
Another dead Indian on the street today,
brother, another 'misunderstanding' with a cop –
he had a knife,
he was a carver,
he was Indian
he was alive
that's still a crime in this day and age.
He was alive,

sometimes just barely,
half deaf, brain soaked in alcohol,
but his fingers
could still read wood.
Today he bled on the street
he bled on the street
he bled on the street
he bled out
on
the street,
the curves of an old design
spilled out of his body –
and when I heard,
all I could do was cry.

What's a few more tears, brother,
in this land with all the marrow sucked out?
Just the memory of your big swollen hands
holding mine, the words of a blessing
slipping from your mouth
onto my bowed, lost-daughter head.
All you had left to give
the last time we met
and I took it.
Now I'll have to carry it with me
the rest of my sorry ass Indian life,
remember how hard you worked
to recall the words,
remember you:
remember where the Indians gather, wait,
on the downtown streets,
in the parks
on the benches,
by the Market –
remember I can't ever run away
from this love.

two

Education

Poverty 101

Poor hearts rattle paper cups on the sidewalk,
limp past in three-inch stilettos –

I've been studying you; your life is my research.
Primitive Disparities: The Love Lives of Poor Urban Indians –

I've been undercover, incognito, watching the way
unrequited love burns holes in your pockets.

You've got more lust than sense, you know that?
Every penny supports some lover's illegal habit,

makes bail for an unfaithful bastard who squandered
his affections on get-love-quick schemes in Florida.

Why do you keep falling for counterfeit tenderness?
Why do you love under the table all your lives,

operate on the barter system, do the loving
no one else wants to do? It just leads you back

to St. Leo's kitchen after 40 hour work weeks,
scrounging for a meal, recycling the same cheap passion

till it's threadbare. I've seen you. Off the grid, off the map,
you moonlight with coyotes just to buy enough gas

for the next rendezvous. I've heard you, poor hearts,
fluttering hard like thin faded prayer flags after

the city has been evacuated. I was there,
remember? – someone offered me bus fare

after the storm, wrapped me in an old red sweater.
I must have really looked the part, eh? Don't believe it.

I'm not one of you. I've got plenty of love.
My heart's not stripped bare. This paper cup? A prop.

I can go home anytime I want.

$10 An Hour

No benefits, no sick leave. You don't see me. You won't remember me if you do. I'm a bucket full of Pledge, PineSol, sponges with scratchy edges. You don't see me vacuum, dust knick knacks, scrub your tub, your toilet. I'll mop hardwood floors with water and vinegar, on hands and knees if that's what you like. I wash your crusty dishes, throw out your Big Gulp cups, sweep up baby's spilled Cheerios. You don't see me pull your teenage son's pornography out from under the playroom sofa, kneel before your moldy vegetable bins in silent attention. I feed the surviving goldfish, scrape out the cat box, empty trash baskets from the master bedroom: used condoms, torn pantyhose, nail clippings, pages ripped from a spiral notebook: "Why did I ever sleep with Jack? What was I thinking?" I polish the locked case beside your bed; carved out of dark wood, it smells of weed and patchouli. You don't see me tidy up your secrets, smooth out the wrinkles of your life. I'm the dark woman with a thick black braid, walking down your driveway at the end of a long week. The gardeners and lawn boys from Oaxaca and Guatemala give me their eyes, a silent nod. I think about the corn plant growing in the gap between the edge of the linoleum and the baseboard of your kitchen sink: so green, so exuberant, so illegal.

Swimming Lessons

Only a thin steel strand of shame
prevents you from lunging forward,
plunging into the cool waters
of someone's heart. Your need

is absolute, devoted, Olympic.
No lane lines, no timer, no lifeguard.
Full-on, frontal, feral desire
to challenge every record.

Someone left the gate open.
The springboard calls your name.
Freestroke, backstroke, breaststroke,
butterfly – your body wants to try them all.

You long for, you lean out:
a swimmer crouched on the blocks,
rapturous face hovering
above a long turquoise body.

The Aubade's Apprentice

We kiss goodbye in an abandoned luggage area; you inch up the escalator towards your gate, I catch a bus back to Westwood - still pitch black out, the driver (in a silver sequined Santa hat, talking to her girlfriend via Bluetooth) speeds us down Olympic under Jurassic palms, tiny stars, a lumbering full moon heading for home like a tired old bear;

sole passenger, I watch ghost SUVs and Ferraris drive through each other on Santa Monica Boulevard, step off at Kinross, 5:45 a.m., walk home a mile in the dark with a quiet Dawn thinking about the color rose but not quite done with indigo yet; in the doorway of a Persian market a man curls up, only the wispy top of his head crowning out of gray blankets, nearby, another man walks in tight circles on the sidewalk, wailing grief and calamity;

he's maybe 60 years old, bushy beard, wild gray hair, jeans matted against thin legs, his several long-sleeved shirts flapping, flying, he sobs and sobs words I can't understand, I don't feel safe enough to stop, dig out money for him, perhaps that's the last thing he wants anyway - I think he just needs his mommy; I imagine her cradling his dear head against her shoulder, the way I stroked your head last night in the dark, unable to sleep before you went away;

then the light changes, I cross the street, turn left at the glass and stone synagogue, right across the bent knees of fig trees; keep walking, past the landlord's perfectly cut green lawn, past his dented Lexus, unlock the bougainvillea'd garden gate, inhale soft tang of ripening oranges on the tree beside my solitary door, step inside just before the sun lights up lonely Moroni on the temple a few blocks to the east:

sound that golden trumpet, angel, bring on the savior, any messiah, before my heart falls down into the sea.

Clementines For Beginners

Let your thumbs find the fruit's top dimple,
apply pressure cleanly, firmly.

Work the skin off in a ragged spiral,
separate flare from the pale sunrise within.

Gather up the long curl of rind,
turn it tight and snug, coy center peeking out.

Leave a Clementine rose
like a love letter on the table.

Now, praise the cleverness of secret compartments.
Raise the Clementine's luminous body

on the tips of your fingers, moist,
undressed: pluck the first sacrificial

half-moon from its sisters
with dreamy dedication:

tongue this plump flame til it bursts,
lush firecracker in the glorious dark of your mouth.

Ten Things I Know About Betrayal

1. Betrayal is the bitch
   that keeps on giving.

2. Betrayal has the teeth
   of a piranha and knows
   how to use them.

3. Betrayal's teeth
   are keys
   that unlock the cage
   of your shame -
   fling you, naked
   and bleeding,
   onto the streets
   at high noon.

4. Asphalt is hard.

5. Other names
   for Betrayal include
   Griefslut, Skeleton-Chewer,
   Revelation.

6. There will be scars.

7. You will have nightmares.

8. You cannot escape
   Betrayal. You can
   only release her
   like the last
   broken notes
   of a song.

9. You cannot forgive
   Betrayal. But you
   can expel her
   with all the grief
   of a woman
   birthing
   a stillborn –

10. You are Betrayal's bitch
    until the day
    you set her free.

Quickening: A Catalog of Desire

My lust is animal, some mystery all skin
all the time – no fur, no feathers, no scales –
dolphin sleek, seal smooth, shell slick. Oh,
she is press, glide, linger, slide, all
mouth and teeth, hot
wet tongue, longing, saliva, terror.

Your lust is mountain range, height past terror,
alder, ash, oak – amber sap beads on rough skin –
she is towering rush, rise, round. Hot
summer days, she is a cool granite ledge to scale,
tall grasses ripening green, fertile, hard, all
seed - breath - pulse - oh –

Our lust is song, dark ululation, steady beat, oh
heart's battlecry – holy terror –
she is medicine, solstice, ceremony, all
sage, grief and stretched drum skin.
She is the balance of scales,
circled dancers, winter stories, close heat.

My lust is ocean: salt and fury, hot
gulf streams, spiraled – no age, no language, oh –
she is unknown memory, leap, blue scales.
She is bottomless trench, monster-breeder, terrorist:
deathless origin of tsunami, skin
flayer, sand creature, devours all.

Your lust is stone: obsidian, basalt, all
splintered, jagged – my dagger, shiv, still hot –
wait and hum, stalking beneath earth's skin.

She is eons, pressure, ancient, oh,
glistening veined terror,
sheer ebony cliff I can't scale.

Our lust is a map, drawn exactly to scale,
glacial lakes, wandering rivers -- landmarks all
rolled up, creased, torn history of terrorism,
she is hand-lettered, jeweled greens and blues, ink hot
as blood, cave entrances, echoes
etched on raw scraped deerskin.

This lust, she is half flesh/half scales, sirena, hot-
blooded in a cold salt sea, sweat song, oh,
steel terror, she tattoos herself on our skin.

Primitive Uses for Poetic Forms

The Poet is a subversive barbarian at the city gates. . .
                     – LAWRENCE FERLINGHETTI

I dress in the skins of sonnets,
wear thin couplets for shoes.

I approach your gates
with my free verse held high

to a heathen god. I sing
with a voice like a fierce pantoum

looking for a mate, smell of smoke
from fires stoked with the dry bones

of villanelles. My feral hair bristles
like an ekphrastic pelt.

From my bag of gutted metaphor
I draw out words round as riverstones,

one by one fit them into my slingshot,
send them soaring like the heads of captives

over your gates into city streets.
What will you do with such ammunition?

Will you set the words into mortar,
build a steep stairway to the top of the gate,

escape with me? Will you collect the stones
where they fall to earth, drill holes, string

a necklace to wear around your neck
- talisman against the ruined regime?

Or will you kick them out of your path, listen
to the syllables stutter into the gutter,

tell yourself, "I can't go home smelling of terza rima"?
This is our ancient game: I rattle your cage.

You pretend not to hear. But at night,
you can't sleep: it is raining words.

Eating a Mountain

You stand in the kitchen, cut
up a buck that a friend
shot for us. I watch you trim,
slice, decide: this is stir fry,
this is steak, this is stew.
These are treats for long-suffering
dogs on the porch, panting. Oh,

we are rich! I rinse, pack,
mark the cuts, this beautiful
deep red velvety offering.
Eating this deer means
eating this mountain:
acorns, ash, beech, dogwood,
maple, oak, willow, autumn olive;

means devouring witch hazel, pine,
lichens, mushrooms, wild grape,
fiddleheads, honeysuckle,
poison ivy, crown vetch,
clover; means nibbling wild onion,
ragweed, beggar's lice, Junegrass,
raspberry cane, paw-paws,

crispy green chickweed,
and so you give the meat
your most honest attention,
dedicate your sharpest blade –
carve up that deer with gratitude,
artistry, prayer, render a wild, sacred animal
into wild, sacred sustenance.

How we eat this deer is a debt
that comes due on the day
we let this mountain
eat us.

Marriage Proposal

FOR MARGO

The cistern pump is broken,
our old Shepherd has a tumor
on his spleen, your father is dying,
our long steep muddy road
is nearly impassable and needs
expensive grading and gravel.
You're simultaneously planning
this year's gardens and major
cervical spine surgery in June (what
the fuck are you thinking?).
Nobody's showering this morning
or even flushing the toilet,
which seems strangely symbolic.
You're on the phone with your sister,
making unexpected travel plans
to visit your dad. Window seat,
or aisle? 30 minute connection?
No problem. (Uh-oh.) I'm in bed
nursing a second cup of tea;
three sets of student papers on my desk,
two essays of my own due,
a daughter in college long past
her tuition benefit, and somewhere,
a partridge in a pear tree. Together
you and I don't even equal one
healthy person but hey, that's
one helluva nice collection
of pain pills, we've still got
health insurance and most
of our teeth. And the Christian

Right is worried we might want
to get married?
Late last night
when I crawled into bed, you
hugged me in your sleep.

Wolf Lullaby

You're out there just beyond the edge of firelight –
trembling, wounded, ears notched, flickering

with the sting of insects attracted to blood. Silently,
your tongue licks the slow seeping scratches

on your paws, strains to reach cuts buried
in the thick pelt of your back. You think I don't see you

but I have learned that slope of canted hip, sickle
of ragged claw, faint whine in the back

of your throat. I'm in no hurry, wolf. I'm in no rush.
When this fire burns down I'll still be here,

my arms open, my belly begging
for your teeth. When you come to devour

me, I'll welcome you into my body:
your howl the only heart I need.

three

faith

My Father Talks to God

In the name of the Father, and of the Son, and of the Holy Ghost.
Well. That's the way the nuns taught me, long time ago,
back when I went to Saint Pat's down on Santa Monica Boulevard,
the place I got kicked out of in 8th grade. And I know, I was a bad
kid in those days. Always cheating, swearing, teasing the girls.

But I was just so curious about everything. Was Sister Marie really
bald beneath her head-thingy? I had to find out. I didn't want to do it,
but I had to find out ... she wasn't. That's when I started going
to public school. When I started drinking and messing around

with girls. Lord, do you really think that was punishment enough?
It seemed more like a reward at the time. I remember saying goodbye
to those nuns, thinking how good it would be not to feel that ruler
whacking down on my knuckles ever again ... God, did nuns perform

your work? 'cause a lot of them were just mean, mean to the bone,
and they was all white women who hated us Indians and our street
Spanish, our dark skin, our tortillas for lunch, our gang slang.
Anyways, Heavenly Father, I hope you know I changed.

I'm an old man now – almost eighty! Who'd have thought I'd make it
this far? What with my old man beating us boys for every little thing,
him and our mom fighting till he left; then it was just the four of us boys,
going everywhere, doing everything together. Till that truck hit Richard

one day. I carried him all the way home in my arms but he didn't make it.
Guess that was one time you weren't payin' much attention, huh.
Then the gangs and the car wrecks, being in the Navy, Japs shooting
at me, and all that drinking, those bare-knuckle fights. That long stretch

in San Quentin; didn't think I'd get out of there alive. All the people
I pissed off. Doesn't seem right that I outlasted Michie. Hell,
she was eight years younger'n me too – and a good woman, I shoulda
treated her better but I didn't know what the hell I was doing. Sure,

she had a mouth on her when she was young and man, could she yell
when I'd come home drunk! Ay, I'd still be drunk in the morning
when it was time to go to work, she'd kick me out of the house
without even making me a pinche cup of coffee. I wrecked that pink

Plymouth one time, the one her folks bought for us because of the baby
... yeah, Michie was a good woman, by God she turned herself around
while I was in prison. Went to Community College – she always was smart
like that – got herself a job, held it for what, twenty, twenty-five years?

Retired just a year before she got that lung cancer. Died at our daughter's
house, that baby girl – turned into a grown woman with two kids of
her own. Michie died and I was up North, too old and sick myself
to come say goodbye. No. I really was sick. Anyways I called her, told her

I loved her; she said it back, but I could tell she was rolling her eyes.
Still, I'm sorry it didn't work for us after I got out of prison. Sorry about
beating up my first wife. And my last wife. Anyways it don't matter now.
I set around this apartment, got to Mass for the highlight of my week, God.

I walk right up to the priest, take communion like when I was an altar boy.
Are you listening, God? I'm trying to be a good Catholic now. I may not
believe in you or Heaven, but I sure as hell believe in Hell. Don't want
to end up there. Too many guys I never want to see again. Well.

Time to take my pills, watch some TV, get myself to bed. Glad my pills make me sleepy. I get too many pictures in my head. My dad, standing at the foot of my bed; he wants to see me again. Maybe. Maybe. In the name of the Father, the Son, and Holy Ghost –

this is Alfred, God, Alfred Edward Miranda, remember me – Amen.

Java Woman

"Your mother called. She'd like coffee."
— SPAM SUBJECT LINE IN MY MAILBOX

I bet she would. Probably doesn't have coffee wherever she is. Too ethereal for mugs and steaming liquid. She wouldn't order from that specialty shop anyways. No, just a can of Folgers; preferably the kind you crack with a can opener, releasing that pop of sharp brown ground scent, taking care not to cut fingers on raw metal edges left behind. She had an aluminum coffee pot for much of my childhood, sat right on the propane burner, with a glass knob on top where the coffee boiled up in carmel-colored bubbles. Later, an electric porcelain pot that "perked." Finally one of those Mr. Coffee models, with paper filters and fussy buttons. Didn't matter how it got made. She'd drink it black, no cream, no sugar. "Hard core java," she'd smile tightly. Though she would add cold water if it was too hot, so she could slug it right down. Constant stream of caffeine, that was my mom, sitting at the kitchen table after dinner talking to my dad, or reading alone once he'd left for good. Beside her mug, that red pack of Pall Malls, her butane lighter in its green and black beaded leather jacket. Matched the beaded key chain someone on the Muckleshoot rez sold her. I still have that key chain, all her keys dangling on it, but the leather fringes darkened, aged and fell off one by one, long ago. You can see the wooden elderberry stick inside, the pith still soft after all these years. Coffee, cigarettes, kitchen table. That was happy. What I thought of as happy, for her. And a good, thick book – Jenny or Roots or a Michener saga. Maybe that's where she is these days. Maybe that's heaven. No men, no kids, no booze – just coffee, cigs and someone else's imaginary world open on the table, enveloping her in complicated, mercifully distant drama.

What We Save

Some things not even a mother can save:
innocence. faith. Our children slide out,
leave our bodies for the life that we gave.

We do all we can to make each one brave,
practice the hallowed hallelujah shout;
some songs not even a mother can save.

We can't take it back, this dear tidal wave;
swim hard, dive deep, keep lungs full and devout.
Our bodies hang onto life that we gave

but sometimes DNA codes just won't behave.
Sometimes battle is an old-fashioned rout.
Some hearts not even a mother can save.

Consult doctors, God, money; love-enslaved,
that tidal wave sometimes turns to heart's drought.
Our bodies let go of the life we gave -

there we are, mothers, full of rant and rave,
caught fast between hope and without a doubt:
some children not even a mother can save.
Keep the womb of memory, life. We gave.

Elegy for My Grief

My grief is not a stray puppy hiding beneath the porch,
waiting to be brought inside, wanting warm blankets and table scraps.

My grief is not a freight train, heated iron wheels on iron rails;
no howl dopplering through an empty night.

Not a phantom limb, not arm nor leg nor finger nor foot
still aching to strike or stride, scratch or kick.

Not a bucket of ice-cold bath water shocking me senseless.
Not a knife, not broken shards of glass, not needles of loss.

My grief does not stalk me, hiding around the corner of an anniversary;
it does not grab my ankles from some dusty lair beneath the bed.

My grief gave itself away, one piece here, a couple pieces there.
Fell apart like an old stone wall, melted like unprotected adobe.

My grief turned to sand, trickled back into the river it came from;
my grief found a pinprick in my heart, thin stream fine as spider web,

a slow leak over decades. Amazing how it peters out at the end, isn't it?
The way grief the size of Alaska gnaws itself down to a pile of dust,

a pair of eye glasses, handful of worn stories.
The outline of a body on the floor fades into wood grain.

When I shake my conscience hard like a linen tablecloth,
only a few stale crumbs fly out into the unsuspecting world

and I am, at last, ready to set that table once more.

Blessing the Doubts

Bless you, doubt shiny as copper, creeping
into my pocket full of debts and past-due loans.

And bless you, enthusiastic doubt, you spring monsoon
washing away all reason and linear thought.

Sharp doubt, teach me how to praise fear in new languages, tuck
yourself into my shoe; constant and true as a splinter.

Oh faithful doubt that refuses to desert me, loyal
as a family ghost or demented mascot! Haunt on.

Ragged runaway doubts, let me harbor you on dark
November evenings when every other door stands locked.

I remember you, the one who pants like a seasoned hound;
you keep up, keep your head down, scent your prey.

Bless you especially, dark-eyed doubt whose gaze leads me
to the ledge, pushes me off into impossible.

Dulles Airport, Sunday Night

Waiting for the last flight out to Roanoke
I wander through gray carpet deserts,

up and down stairs, dazed by 3,000 miles
and lack of sleep, still glowing from the tender brush

of Sacramento's air at 5 a.m. on my cheeks
like a mother's goodbye.

I come upon an anonymous corner; a man
kneels, faces the wall on a gray-white rectangle of cloth.

His intention so wholly fills his middle-aged body
I am embarrassed

to interrupt but he gracefully lowers
his forehead to the floor

in singular reverence
and gratitude washes over me

for his devotion.
I walk around the corner,

stand looking out at the dusky tarmac
beneath an almost-indigo sky.

I let go of my suitcase,
open my hands,

try to pray
that unabashedly.

Rosary

Put me on a train, let me ride all the way from San Diego to Sacramento. Let me watch the lands I love unroll like a scroll, a story that keeps opening and opening, rich and full of sky, sand, oaks, hills, ocean, pines, snow. Let me drink in the old voices living there. Let the old knowledge seep back into me. Feast my eyes? I am a glutton! Unable to turn away, not wanting to sleep. Let the train rock me back and forth, jostle me over a rough spot in the track; let the steel wheels beneath the floor whine and sing.

Let the long slow grades ease us down from the mountains like a snake on a summer day, silver scales sparkling in the sun. Put me on a train; let the world shrink down to this one ragged coastline. Let this narrow corridor become the only world that matters.

Rumbling through Los Angeles, I'll look for the dry cement banks of the river we have never forgotten, see homeless souls living in the mouths of drains that haven't seen a drop of water in months. They know what they're doing: blue tarps over the entrance, a battered lawn chair – would I manage as well? If I knew how to pray, I would pray for them, those people who never pray for rain.

San Juan Capistrano, San Fernando Rey de España, Santa Barbara. Let me pass by the adobe missions, the ridiculously renovated, the melting rubble, with tender thoughts for the souls of my ancestors. Like clay and stone, we transform: that is the string of miracles I follow.

Stones

Small stones told their first stories
long ago, wore away each word.
Now they tell the story found
a hundred layers down
when a larger being burst,
gave birth.

Some stones emerge
like tears, spill smooth
and clean. Others chip
into testimonies, scarred
by their violent journey.

The most beautiful stone
lies buried for a thousand storms,
surfaces on the longest day
of the year, heats in the sun
like a speckled egg beneath
a mother hawk's breast.
Tomorrow it will lie once more
beneath the multitudes.

Stones breathe slowly:
draw in air from one century,
let it out in the next.

Some stones bear white lines
crisscrossed maps left behind
by tiny voyagers, love poems
inscribed by creatures
from that molten dimension of desire,
or the work of unseen beings

whose sacred drawings hold
the world together.

Even when fanned out
on a sickle of gray beach
between summer rains,
stones think about becoming –
sand, soil, the grit and grind
of the world's soul.

Stones take to the sky
as iridescent dust on wings;
particles shimmer down
through dusk,
bless our stubborn heads
in the precise place
where the tender spirit enters,
and departs.

Some Years

WITH THANKS TO ADAM ZAGAJEWSKI

It is the year
April bursts into flame:
30,000 acres
of mature oak and pine forest
burn down to ash.
Fires with names
like Rich Hole, Alleghany Tunnels,
Barbours Creek, Shipwreck and Wolf Gap
turn a valley into a crematorium.
The air isn't fit for breathing,
cinders scratch eyeballs, lungs
ache and heave. The bodies of trees
cry down on the earth,
there's no stopping this massacre
and the sky has been abducted
by aliens.

It is the year
May's trees scream
in chorus: 17 year cicadas
emerge out of round holes
in the earth, shed clumsy skins,
find love in the trees.
Males ratchet up, belt out
lust like banshees.
Afterwards their golden bodies
fall to earth in great glorious waves,
dead red eyes staring. Females
slit open branches like wrists,
lap up the sap, lay down their eggs,

disappear –
Magicicada septendecim –
leave behind the brown flags
of death.

It is the year
of the derecho:
June air turns into a brick wall,
crashes down like God's fist.
Trees bend and crack,
trunks shatter like glass
or else lay their crowns down,
kiss the ground, clutch boulders
that rip out anyway –
leave behind craters of open earth,
oaks stretched out on the ground
like beached whales
no longer living in two worlds,
but pulled wholly into air.
Old roots thick as fire hoses
gasp at the sky.

Some years burn you up.
Some years suck you dry.
Some years rip out your heart
and dance on it. Hang on. In these years,
you must think like a phoenix.
Regenerate like a starfish.
Teach your heart it must grow legs,
walk out into the mutilated world
without you.

Why God Made So Many Crows

I know I will travel to heaven in the guts of a crow –
each of us assigned transportation at birth, marked

upon our arrival in smoggy cities, cold mountains,
deserted parking lots. God makes certain no body

is forgotten, no flesh left undigested. A time to live,
a time to die, a time to re-enter Creation through

the lift of blackest feathers. I can pick my crow out
of a crowd despite identical sleek pinions

and clacking black beaks – he's something special, not
like the other trash-picking, dirt-talking, rabble-rousing

wannabes, ganging up on juveniles too big for the nest,
too thin for the flock. He stands alone on the bright yellow

centerline, guards fresh possum guts, sticky raccoon entrails,
nicely splattered deer brains; doesn't flinch as I draw closer

in my big steel and plastic boat on wheels. I can't
stare him down; he's just doing his job: recycling

what's too slow, too old, too stupid to live, and I,
I am simply the one he's got his eye on next.

Not today, but thank you, I say as we pass: Keep up
the good work without me, brother.

Faith

Yesterday I saw
wild turkey running
in the road,

fluttering, frantic
for cover; a young deer
dead in the stream.

This morning chainsaws whine
on storm-dropped oaks,
wood smoke tendrils cold air.

You put the garden to bed
with bales of sweet hay
from a barn protected

by an old Dutch design.
All around the outside skin
of our house, spiders pack up

their egg sacks, anchor
the next generation
snug in tight corners,

along ledges,
under flat stones.
In spring, the golden

spiderlings will hatch,
loose newly-spun lines,
catch the next silky gust out –

bet everything they have
that there's a place to anchor
on the other side.

Even the alphabet is precious.
–ADRIENNE RICH

DECOLONIZING THE ALPHABET

1.
Literacy starts with flesh
ripped from the backs of my ancestors,
inscriptions by soldier's whips,
a priest's cudgel, the ranchero's lariat;
scars scrawled at Indian Boarding Schools,
clubs across knuckles, buttocks, shoulders, knees:
learn this holy language, it will make you
civilized.

Literate, litteratus: marked with letters. Scars
carved in wide lines left by leather straps.
Scars sketched thin but deep,
cowhide tipped with sharp iron barbs.
Scars, thick as rope, fattened on infection and fever:
alphabet of blood and bruises.

2.
A, broken pieces of our lives they call artifacts. B, iron bound
around our wrists. C, the cupped hand that covets. D, demonic grin
at our cries of pain. E, the rake to excise weeds from the earth;
F, the key to padlocked fences. G, the open maw of genocide.
H, locked gate of our hearts; I, government-issued identification
required. J, the shovel that jabs at our graves; K, a boot kicking us
into the next relocation; L, the club that lashes us into submission.
M, the path of our migration off your maps; N, for nits (they make
lice). O: we have no word for ownership. P, a salute between sol-
diers; Q, the quick breath of hope slipping out. R, the rifle to hold
back the ravenous savages; S, slick blood sliding down a cheek.
T, the tree where they hang us. U, go back where you came from; V,

the plow that vindicates murder. W, barbed wire fangs of a witch. X
for the crucifix that could not save us from itself; Y, yes from a
forked tongue. Z, the place they aim to drive us: Zero.

3.
Alphabets of terror, of adobe, our own prison made from the mud of
our own land, mixed with our own feet. The alphabets of walls: this
alphabet we never asked for, 'given' to us like a parasite in our guts,
shackle around our wrist, gag in our mouths. This alphabet like a
cattle brand. This alphabet meant to strangle us - the umbilical cord
of a mother who hates her bastard child.

Uppercase, lowercase, block letter, cursive, all clatter chatter like
teeth, nip at our flesh, taste us, gnaw at us with scythed edges and
wide grinding surfaces. They strip us of our names. Eat through
skin, muscle, bone; head for the marrow, spread through our skele-
tons. Poison that erases memory, replaces it with obedience.

This alphabet that some of us endure. Learn to bear. Our skin
grows more callused. Our scars become our art. This alphabet we
chew on as starving children chew on grass or suck on pebbles.
This alphabet of conquest that was never meant to serve us, speak
for us, fight for us. This alphabet of razor wire we take into our
hands, twist to our own bloody testimonies. This alphabet that
gnawed its way inside of us; a tool, a weapon we use to carve our
way back out.

4.
You ripped out our tongues:
language, prayer, song, medicine, history,
home. You shoved this alphabet down our throats
so we could write the names you gave us
on treaties, add the names of our children
and our dead to the back of a Bible,
keep track of our numbers, remember our place.
A special kind of literacy that grants us the right

to read your grocery lists, sweat in your factories,
drive your trucks, pay taxes, but never
tell our own stories.

You never thought we could
wield these letters for ourselves,
write our humanity, make new songs,
become lawyers or poets – redefine words
like warrior or strategy.

This alphabet. This charm.
This code of conquest made into codex
of creation. You never thought
we could appropriate your weapon,
re-shape it into a tool with our torn hands, carry it
on our scarred backs all this distance,
all these years.

You never imagined this:
your alphabet betraying its duty,
defecting to our cause, going Native,
becoming indigenous to this land because
we give birth to it with our blood. No wonder
our books are banned, our children told
don't read that, don't write that. Don't read,
don't write. Don't.
We've learned too much.

You want your alphabet returned to you;
all 26 letters, unharmed, unchanged,
well-behaved letters that don't curse
or tell ugly truths.

Our Storyteller, she tried to warn you.
Like rape, like syphilis, like small pox,
like massacre: that alphabet

is already turned loose.
It's already coming.
It's alive.
It's ours.

We will not give it back.

ACKNOWLEDGMENTS

THIS BOOK exists thanks to the generosity and care of many: human and non-human, animate and inanimate, living and transformed. Thank you Margo Solod, for endless cups of tea, solitude, critique, and bottomless faith. Thanks also to Luis Rodriguez for hanging onto a manuscript handed to him in the midst of AWP chaos and seeing its potential, to Anita Endrezze for her collage-work that speaks my language, and to Kimberly Blaeser, Ernestine Saankalaxt' Hayes, Luisa A. Igloria, and Mona Susan Power for taking precious time out of their own own writing lives to read and write about my work. Thank you to the Third Floor Poets & Scholars: Lesley Wheeler, Holly Pickett and Leah Green, for their energy and enthusiasm when my own poetry-spirit flagged. Thank you to Suzanne Keen, voice of clarity and reason. Thank you to Washington and Lee's Summer Lenfest Research Grants, which powered many of these poems onto the page, and to Macondistas todos but especially Rosalind Bell, Maria Limón, Michelle Otero, Linda Rodriguez and Ire'ne Lara Silva. Thank you to Big House Mountain, Cuttyhunk Island, Virginia Center for the Creative Arts, East Preston Street. Big hugs to Lady, Chance and Mandy. And as always, nimasianexelpasaleki to my Ancestors and family: love knows no boundaries, not even time or anger or distance. - dm

The following poems have been published in these journals:

"Clementines for Beginners" (as "Clementines") in *Sovereign Erotics: An Anthology of Two-Spirit Literature*. U of Arizona Press, 2011.

"Eating a Mountain," in *Natural Bridge Literary Journal,* 2011; *Ecopoetry: A Contemporary American Anthology,* Trinity UP, 2012; and *Platte Valley Review* 2012.

"Faith" in *Spring Salmon, Hurry to Me*. Heyday Books, 2008.

"Mnemonic," in *New California Writing 2012*. Heyday Books, 2012.

"Oral History," in *Women Write Resistance: Poets Resist Gender Violence.* Blue Light Press, 2013.

"Quickening: A Catalog of Desire" (as "Quickening") in *Platte Valley Review.* Vol. 32, Issue 2, 2011 and the anthology *Obsession: Sestinas for the 21st Century,* forthcoming.

"Raised By Humans" in *Platte Valley Review.* Vol. 32, Issue 2, 2011.

"Why God Made So Many Crows" (as "My Crow"), in *A Bird Black As the Sun: California Poets on Crows and Ravens.* Green Poets Press, 2011

About the Author

DEBORAH A. MIRANDA is an enrolled member of the Ohlone-Costanoan Esselen Nation of the Greater Monterey Bay Area, and author of the mixed-genre *Bad Indians: A Tribal Memoir,* winner of an IPPY Gold Medal for Autobiography/Memoir. She has also published two poetry collections (*Indian Cartography* and *The Zen of La Llorona*) and co-edited *Sovereign Erotics: An Anthology of Two Spirit Literature.*

Currently Deborah is John Lucian Smith Jr. Memorial Term Professor of English at Washington and Lee University in Lexington, Virginia where she teaches creative writing and literature. Most recently, Deborah has been working on a collection of essays exploring the lives of Indians at Carmel Mission during the post-secularization era, as well as a collection of poems in the voices of the twenty-one California missions.